Composition Notebook

R

Made in United States
Orlando, FL
14 July 2025

62951696R00063